Copyright © 2023 by Herman Strange (Author)

All rights reserved. This book or any portion thereof may not be reproduced or used in any manner whatsoever without the express written permission of the publisher except for the use of brief quotations in a book review.

This book is copyright protected. This is only for personal use. You cannot amend, distributor, sell, use, quote or paraphrase any part or the content within this book without the consent of the author. Please note the information contained within this document is for educational and entertainment purposes only. Every attempt has been made to provide accurate, up to date and reliable complete information. No warranties of any kind are expressed or implied.

Readers acknowledge that the author is not engaging in the rendering of legal, financial, medical or professional advice. The content of this book has been derived from various sources. Please consult a licensed professional before attempting any techniques outlined in this book.

By reading this document, the readers agree that under no circumstances are the author responsible for any losses, direct or indirect, which are incurred as a result of the use of information contained within this document, including but not limited to errors, omissions or inaccuracies.

Thank you very much for reading this book.

Title: Machines that Think-History of Artificial Intelligence
Subtitle: Navigating the Ethical, Societal, and Technical Dimensions of AI Development

Series: Rise of Cognitive Computing: AI Evolution from Origins to Adoption
Author: Herman Strange

Table of Contents

Introduction 5
  Definition of AI and its applications 5
  The purpose of the book 7
  Brief overview of the chapters 9

Chapter 1: The Origins of AI 12
  The early history of AI and its pioneers 12
  The Turing Test and the imitation game 14
  The Dartmouth Conference and the birth of AI research 16
  The first AI programs and applications 18

Chapter 2: The Rise of Machine Learning 20
  The development of machine learning algorithms 20
  The perceptron and linear classification 23
  Backpropagation and multi-layer neural networks 25
  Support vector machines and kernel methods 27

Chapter 3: The Emergence of Deep Learning 29
  The development of deep learning algorithms 29
  Convolutional neural networks and image recognition . 32
  Recurrent neural networks and natural language processing 34
  Reinforcement learning and game playing 36

Chapter 4: The Dark Side of AI 39
  Potential risks and challenges presented by AI 39
  Job displacement and automation 42

Bias in AI decision-making 45

Privacy and security concerns 49

Chapter 5: The Societal Impact of AI **54**

The impact of AI on employment and the economy 54

AI in education and healthcare 57

AI and social inequality 60

AI and the environment 63

Chapter 6: The Ethical Implications of AI **68**

The ethical and moral implications of AI 68

Bias and fairness in AI decision-making 71

The role of humans in AI decision-making 74

The ethics of creating autonomous AI systems 77

Conclusion **80**

The potential future of AI and its impact on society 80

The need for continued research and development in AI 83

The importance of ethical and responsible AI development and use 85

Final thoughts and recommendations for further reading 88

Potential References **91**

Introduction
Definition of AI and its applications

Artificial Intelligence (AI) is a broad field that encompasses a wide range of technologies and techniques used to create machines that can learn, reason, and make decisions like humans. AI is built upon the principles of computer science, mathematics, statistics, and cognitive psychology, and it has evolved significantly since its inception in the mid-20th century.

At its core, AI is all about creating intelligent machines that can perform tasks that typically require human-like intelligence, such as recognizing speech, understanding natural language, and making predictions based on data. These machines can also learn and adapt over time, which makes them useful for a wide range of applications.

Some common applications of AI include:

1. Natural Language Processing (NLP): NLP is a field of AI that focuses on teaching machines to understand and interpret human language. This technology is used in applications such as virtual assistants, chatbots, and language translation software.

2. Computer Vision: Computer vision is a branch of AI that enables machines to "see" and interpret the world

around them. This technology is used in applications such as facial recognition, object detection, and self-driving cars.

3. Machine Learning: Machine learning is a technique used in AI to enable machines to learn from data without being explicitly programmed. This technology is used in applications such as fraud detection, recommendation systems, and predictive maintenance.

4. Robotics: Robotics is a field of AI that focuses on creating intelligent machines that can interact with the physical world. This technology is used in applications such as manufacturing, healthcare, and transportation.

Overall, AI has the potential to revolutionize the way we live and work. By creating machines that can learn, reason, and make decisions like humans, we can automate repetitive tasks, improve efficiency, and make better decisions based on data. However, as AI becomes more advanced, it also raises ethical and societal concerns that must be addressed.

The purpose of the book

The purpose of this book, Machines that Think-History of Artificial Intelligence: Navigating the Ethical, Societal, and Technical Dimensions of AI Development, is to provide a comprehensive overview of the history of artificial intelligence, its current state, and its potential future. This book aims to be accessible to both technical and non-technical readers, providing a broad understanding of the field and its applications.

One of the primary goals of this book is to examine the ethical and societal challenges that come with the development of autonomous systems and intelligent machines. As AI technology continues to advance, there are growing concerns about the impact it may have on society, including potential job displacement, biased decision-making, and threats to privacy and security. This book will explore these issues in depth, highlighting potential risks and presenting possible solutions.

Another goal of this book is to provide readers with a clear understanding of the technical aspects of AI. This includes an overview of various machine learning and deep learning algorithms, as well as an explanation of how they work and their potential applications. By presenting this information in an accessible way, this book aims to help readers understand the technical side of AI without requiring a background in computer science or mathematics.

Overall, the purpose of this book is to provide readers with a comprehensive understanding of the history, current state, and potential future of artificial intelligence, while also examining the ethical and societal challenges that come with its development. By exploring these topics in depth, this book aims to inform readers about the many facets of AI and help them navigate the complex and rapidly evolving landscape of this exciting field.

Brief overview of the chapters

The brief overview of the chapters section provides readers with a summary of what they can expect from the book. This section aims to give readers an idea of the topics that will be covered in each chapter and to help them understand the structure of the book.

Chapter 1, "The Origins of AI," begins with the early history of AI and its pioneers. This chapter discusses the development of the Turing Test and the imitation game, which were important in shaping the early ideas of AI. The Dartmouth Conference is also covered, which was a significant event that marked the birth of AI research. Additionally, this chapter will cover the first AI programs and applications.

Chapter 2, "The Rise of Machine Learning," covers the development of machine learning algorithms. This chapter includes discussions of the perceptron and linear classification, backpropagation and multi-layer neural networks, and support vector machines and kernel methods. These algorithms played an important role in shaping the future of AI and made significant contributions to the development of intelligent machines.

Chapter 3, "The Emergence of Deep Learning," focuses on the development of deep learning algorithms.

This chapter will cover convolutional neural networks and image recognition, recurrent neural networks and natural language processing, and reinforcement learning and game playing. These algorithms are some of the most significant advancements in AI and have contributed to the development of intelligent systems that can learn, recognize patterns, and make decisions.

Chapter 4, "The Dark Side of AI," explores the potential risks and challenges presented by AI. This chapter includes discussions of job displacement and automation, bias in AI decision-making, and privacy and security concerns. It is important to understand these challenges to develop ethical and responsible AI systems that can benefit society.

Chapter 5, "The Societal Impact of AI," discusses the impact of AI on employment and the economy, AI in education and healthcare, AI and social inequality, and AI and the environment. It is important to understand the societal impact of AI to develop ethical and responsible AI systems that can benefit society.

Chapter 6, "The Ethical Implications of AI," examines the ethical and moral implications of AI. This chapter includes discussions of bias and fairness in AI decision-making, the role of humans in AI decision-making, and the ethics of creating autonomous AI systems. It is important to understand the ethical implications of AI to develop responsible and beneficial AI systems.

In the conclusion, "The potential future of AI and its impact on society" is discussed. This chapter covers the need for continued research and development in AI, the importance of ethical and responsible AI development and use, and final thoughts and recommendations for further reading. The potential future of AI is exciting and will continue to shape society in ways that we cannot yet fully predict.

Chapter 1: The Origins of AI
The early history of AI and its pioneers

The concept of artificial intelligence (AI) is not a recent one, and it has its roots in ancient times when people dreamed of creating machines that could think and work like humans. However, the modern-day AI we know of today owes its existence to the pioneers of AI who laid the foundation for AI research.

One of the earliest known attempts to create a machine that could think was made by Greek mathematician Archytas in the 4th century BC. He constructed a mechanical bird that could fly and was powered by steam. The bird was controlled by a system of pulleys and cables and could flap its wings and make sounds like a real bird.

The 17th-century philosopher and mathematician René Descartes proposed the idea of mechanizing the human thought process, which laid the groundwork for the development of AI. In the 18th century, the French mathematician Jean-Jacques d'Alembert developed a mechanical calculator that could perform basic arithmetic operations.

The early 19th century saw the development of the first programmable machine, the Analytical Engine, by the English mathematician Charles Babbage. Although the machine was never built, it was the first design for a programmable computer.

In the 20th century, the concept of AI started to take shape. In 1950, computer pioneer Alan Turing proposed the famous Turing Test, which was designed to test a machine's ability to exhibit intelligent behavior that is indistinguishable from that of a human. This led to the development of the first AI programs and applications.

Other pioneers in the early history of AI include John McCarthy, Marvin Minsky, Claude Shannon, and Nathaniel Rochester. They conducted research in AI and founded the field of AI research. They organized the Dartmouth Conference in 1956, which is considered the birthplace of AI research.

In conclusion, the early history of AI is a fascinating tale of innovation and creativity. The pioneers of AI laid the foundation for the development of AI as we know it today. They paved the way for future generations to build on their work and explore the full potential of AI.

The Turing Test and the imitation game

The Turing Test, also known as the imitation game, is a concept proposed by the British mathematician and computer scientist, Alan Turing, in his 1950 paper titled "Computing Machinery and Intelligence." The test was designed to evaluate a machine's ability to exhibit intelligent behavior that is indistinguishable from that of a human.

The basic idea of the Turing Test is that a human judge would communicate with a machine and a human via a text-based interface. The machine would try to convince the judge that it is human, while the human would also attempt to convince the judge of their humanity. If the machine can consistently fool the human judge into believing it is a human, then it passes the Turing Test.

The Turing Test was significant because it provided a standard for evaluating the intelligence of a machine. Turing argued that if a machine could successfully pass the Turing Test, then it would be reasonable to say that the machine possesses human-like intelligence.

The Turing Test has been widely used as a benchmark for evaluating the progress of AI research. In 1991, the Loebner Prize was established as an annual competition that awards a prize to the computer program that comes closest to passing the Turing Test. The prize money has increased over the years, with a current prize of $100,000.

While the Turing Test remains an important benchmark for evaluating AI, it has also been the subject of criticism. Some argue that it places too much emphasis on language-based communication, and that there are other aspects of intelligence that are not captured by the test.

Nevertheless, the Turing Test remains an important concept in the history of AI, and it has influenced the development of natural language processing, machine learning, and other AI-related fields.

The Dartmouth Conference and the birth of AI research

In 1956, a group of researchers from different fields gathered for a summer workshop at Dartmouth College in New Hampshire to discuss the potential of machines to exhibit human-like intelligence. This event marked the birth of AI research as a distinct field of study.

The Dartmouth Conference was organized by John McCarthy, Marvin Minsky, Nathaniel Rochester, and Claude Shannon. They envisioned a multidisciplinary approach to AI research that involved not only computer scientists but also psychologists, linguists, and other experts.

The conference was attended by a small but influential group of researchers, including McCarthy and Minsky, who became two of the most important figures in the early development of AI. During the conference, the attendees discussed a wide range of topics related to AI, including problem-solving, learning, and natural language processing.

One of the main outcomes of the conference was the proposal of the Dartmouth Conference Proposal, which outlined the goals and objectives of AI research. The proposal called for the development of machines that could simulate human thought and problem-solving abilities. It also emphasized the importance of programming languages and algorithms for the creation of intelligent machines.

The Dartmouth Conference had a significant impact on the development of AI research. It provided a platform for researchers to share their ideas and collaborate on new approaches to AI. The conference also led to the creation of the first AI programs, such as the Logic Theorist and the General Problem Solver.

However, the initial optimism about the potential of AI was soon tempered by the realization that creating intelligent machines was much more challenging than originally thought. Despite this, the legacy of the Dartmouth Conference lives on in the ongoing pursuit of developing machines that can exhibit human-like intelligence.

The first AI programs and applications

The development of AI progressed rapidly after the Dartmouth Conference. Researchers began experimenting with new techniques for machine learning and problem-solving. By the late 1950s, a number of groundbreaking AI programs and applications had been developed.

One of the earliest AI programs was called the Logic Theorist, developed by Allen Newell and J.C. Shaw in 1956. The program was designed to prove mathematical theorems using symbolic logic. It was able to prove 38 out of the first 52 theorems in Whitehead and Russell's Principia Mathematica, demonstrating the potential of AI for problem-solving.

Another influential program from this period was the General Problem Solver (GPS), developed by Newell and Herbert Simon in 1957. GPS was designed to solve a wide range of problems by searching through a problem space and applying problem-solving heuristics. The program was able to solve problems in areas such as geometry, algebra, and logic, demonstrating the power of general-purpose problem-solving algorithms.

Other notable AI programs from this period include the Machine Translation project, led by Warren Weaver and developed at IBM in the late 1950s, which aimed to automatically translate between languages, and the Shakey robot, developed by the Stanford Research Institute in the late 1960s, which was capable of navigating its environment and performing simple tasks.

The early AI applications were primarily focused on symbolic reasoning and problem-solving. However, researchers began exploring other areas such as natural language processing, computer vision, and robotics. The development of these areas led to new and more sophisticated AI applications in later years.

Overall, the development of the first AI programs and applications marked a significant milestone in the history of AI. These early programs demonstrated the potential of AI for problem-solving and led to further research and development in the field.

Chapter 2: The Rise of Machine Learning
The development of machine learning algorithms

Machine learning is a subfield of artificial intelligence (AI) that focuses on the development of algorithms and models that enable machines to learn and make predictions or decisions without being explicitly programmed. Machine learning has become one of the most rapidly advancing fields of study in the modern era, with an ever-increasing number of applications and practical uses.

At its core, machine learning is about teaching machines to recognize patterns and make predictions based on those patterns. To accomplish this, machine learning algorithms require large amounts of data to be trained on. The process of training a machine learning model involves feeding it with a dataset and adjusting its parameters until it can accurately predict outcomes on new data. There are two broad types of machine learning algorithms: supervised learning and unsupervised learning.

Supervised learning is the most common form of machine learning and involves providing the machine learning algorithm with a labeled dataset, where each data point is labeled with the correct output or prediction. The algorithm then learns to map inputs to outputs by adjusting its internal parameters until it can accurately predict outputs on new, unseen data.

Unsupervised learning, on the other hand, involves providing the machine learning algorithm with an unlabeled dataset and asking it to find patterns or groupings in the data. The algorithm must then identify the underlying structure of the data and group similar data points together.

One of the earliest examples of machine learning was the development of decision tree algorithms in the 1960s. These algorithms were used to classify data into discrete categories based on a series of if-then rules. Another early breakthrough in machine learning was the development of the nearest neighbor algorithm, which could classify data points based on their proximity to known examples.

In the 1980s and 1990s, machine learning began to make significant strides in areas such as computer vision, natural language processing, and speech recognition. This led to the development of algorithms such as the perceptron and support vector machines, which could classify data points into multiple categories with high accuracy.

More recently, deep learning has emerged as a major subfield of machine learning, characterized by the use of neural networks with many layers. Deep learning has proven particularly effective in areas such as image recognition and natural language processing, and has been used to develop cutting-edge applications such as self-driving cars and virtual assistants.

In summary, the development of machine learning algorithms has played a crucial role in the evolution of artificial intelligence. With the ability to recognize patterns and make predictions based on those patterns, machines are now able to accomplish tasks that were once thought to be the exclusive domain of human intelligence.

The perceptron and linear classification

The perceptron is a fundamental concept in the field of machine learning. It is a type of artificial neuron that was introduced in 1957 by Frank Rosenblatt, an American psychologist and computer scientist. The perceptron is a single-layer neural network that is capable of learning linearly separable patterns. It takes in inputs, applies weights to each input, sums the weighted inputs, and then applies a threshold function to produce an output.

The perceptron was designed to solve problems that can be represented as linearly separable patterns, such as pattern recognition and classification problems. It works by adjusting the weights assigned to each input until it can correctly classify the inputs. The perceptron learning rule involves adjusting the weights after each iteration until the algorithm converges on a solution.

One of the most famous applications of the perceptron was in the recognition of handwritten digits. In the 1960s, researchers at the Stanford Research Institute trained a perceptron on a dataset of handwritten digits and achieved an accuracy of around 80%. This was considered a significant breakthrough at the time, and it demonstrated the potential of machine learning for pattern recognition tasks.

Linear classification is another important concept in machine learning. It refers to the process of dividing a dataset into two or more classes based on a linear decision boundary. Linear classification algorithms are used extensively in machine learning for tasks such as image classification, spam detection, and sentiment analysis.

The perceptron is a linear classification algorithm because it can only learn linearly separable patterns. However, there are other algorithms that can learn more complex patterns, such as support vector machines and neural networks. Nonetheless, the perceptron remains an important concept in the field of machine learning, and it paved the way for many of the developments that followed.

Backpropagation and multi-layer neural networks

Backpropagation is a key algorithm in training multi-layer neural networks, which has been a critical development in the rise of machine learning. The algorithm was first introduced in the 1970s, but it was not widely used until the 1980s and 1990s when computational power increased.

Backpropagation is a supervised learning method used to adjust the weights of the connections in a neural network, so that the network can learn from the input data and produce accurate output predictions. It is based on the principle of gradient descent, which involves computing the gradient of the loss function with respect to the weights of the neural network. The gradient provides information about how the weights should be adjusted to reduce the error between the predicted output and the actual output.

The backpropagation algorithm involves two phases: forward propagation and backward propagation. In the forward propagation phase, the input data is fed through the neural network, and the output is calculated using the current weights. In the backward propagation phase, the error between the predicted output and the actual output is computed, and the weights are adjusted to minimize the error.

Multi-layer neural networks, also known as deep neural networks, have become the most successful machine learning models in recent years, with applications in speech recognition, image classification, and natural language processing. The key advantage of deep neural networks is their ability to learn hierarchical representations of the input data, which enables them to capture complex patterns and relationships.

The use of backpropagation in training deep neural networks has been critical in their success. With the ability to learn from massive amounts of data, deep neural networks have achieved state-of-the-art performance in a variety of tasks, including object recognition, speech recognition, and natural language processing. However, training deep neural networks can be computationally intensive, requiring specialized hardware such as graphics processing units (GPUs) and tensor processing units (TPUs).

The development of backpropagation and multi-layer neural networks has been a major milestone in the history of machine learning, paving the way for the development of more advanced machine learning algorithms such as convolutional neural networks and recurrent neural networks.

Support vector machines and kernel methods

Support vector machines (SVMs) are a powerful class of algorithms used in machine learning for classification and regression analysis. SVMs were introduced by Vladimir Vapnik and his colleagues in the 1990s and have since become a popular method for solving complex classification problems.

At its core, SVM is a binary classification algorithm that attempts to find a hyperplane in a high-dimensional feature space that separates the data into two classes. The hyperplane is chosen so that it maximizes the margin between the two classes, which is defined as the distance between the hyperplane and the nearest data points on either side.

The basic idea behind SVMs is to map the input data into a higher-dimensional feature space where a linear decision boundary can be drawn more easily. This is done using a kernel function, which transforms the input data into a higher-dimensional space without actually computing the coordinates of the data in that space. The most commonly used kernel functions include linear, polynomial, and radial basis function (RBF) kernels.

One of the main advantages of SVMs is that they are able to handle high-dimensional data and can work with both linear and nonlinear classification problems. They also have a strong theoretical foundation and have been proven to work well in practice for a wide range of applications, including image classification, text classification, and bioinformatics.

However, SVMs also have some limitations. They can be computationally expensive to train on large datasets, and the choice of kernel function and hyperparameters can have a significant impact on the performance of the algorithm. Additionally, SVMs are a binary classification algorithm, which means they may not be suitable for problems with more than two classes.

Despite these limitations, SVMs remain an important tool in the machine learning toolkit and have contributed significantly to the rise of machine learning as a field. As researchers continue to develop new algorithms and techniques, it is likely that SVMs will continue to play an important role in the development of more powerful and efficient machine learning models.

Chapter 3: The Emergence of Deep Learning

The development of deep learning algorithms

Deep learning is a subset of machine learning that involves training artificial neural networks to learn from large amounts of data. Deep learning algorithms are designed to automatically learn hierarchical representations of data by stacking multiple layers of interconnected nodes. This enables them to learn more complex patterns and relationships in the data than traditional machine learning algorithms.

The development of deep learning algorithms can be traced back to the 1980s, but it was not until the 2000s and 2010s that they became widely used and achieved state-of-the-art performance on many tasks, such as image and speech recognition, natural language processing, and game playing.

One of the breakthroughs in the development of deep learning was the introduction of the backpropagation algorithm, which allows for efficient training of multi-layer neural networks. Backpropagation involves computing the gradient of the error with respect to the weights of the network and using it to update the weights in the opposite direction of the gradient to minimize the error.

Another important development in deep learning was the introduction of convolutional neural networks (CNNs) by Yann LeCun and colleagues in the 1990s. CNNs are designed to exploit the spatial and temporal structure of data, such as images and videos, by convolving the input with a set of learnable filters to extract local features. This makes them particularly effective for tasks such as image recognition, where the spatial arrangement of pixels is important.

Recurrent neural networks (RNNs) are another type of deep learning algorithm that is well-suited for sequential data, such as speech and text. RNNs maintain an internal state that is updated at each time step based on the input and previous state, allowing them to model long-term dependencies in the data. This makes them particularly effective for tasks such as language translation, where the meaning of a sentence depends on the context of previous words.

In recent years, deep reinforcement learning has emerged as a promising approach for training AI agents to learn to make decisions in complex environments, such as playing video games or controlling robots. Reinforcement learning involves training an agent to maximize a reward signal by interacting with an environment and learning from feedback.

Overall, the development of deep learning algorithms has revolutionized the field of AI and enabled significant advances in many areas. However, these algorithms also pose challenges such as the need for large amounts of data and computing resources, as well as concerns about their interpretability and fairness.

Convolutional neural networks and image recognition

Convolutional neural networks (CNNs) are a type of deep learning algorithm that have revolutionized image recognition tasks. The architecture of a CNN is inspired by the organization of the visual cortex in the brain, with different layers of neurons processing increasingly complex visual features.

In a CNN, the input image is passed through a series of convolutional layers, where each layer learns to detect specific features in the image, such as edges or textures. Each convolutional layer applies a set of filters or kernels to the input image, generating a feature map for each filter. The filters are learned through a process called backpropagation, where the network adjusts the weights of the filters to minimize the error between the predicted and actual outputs.

After the convolutional layers, the output is passed through one or more fully connected layers, which perform the final classification task. The fully connected layers are similar to those in a traditional neural network, where each neuron in the layer is connected to every neuron in the previous layer.

CNNs have achieved state-of-the-art performance on a wide range of image recognition tasks, such as object detection, face recognition, and scene classification. For example, the ImageNet Large Scale Visual Recognition Challenge (ILSVRC) is an annual competition where teams develop algorithms to classify images into 1,000 different object categories. In 2012, a CNN developed by Alex Krizhevsky et al., known as AlexNet, achieved a top-5 error rate of 15.3%, significantly outperforming traditional machine learning algorithms.

Since then, many variations of CNNs have been developed, including architectures like VGG, ResNet, and Inception. These architectures differ in their number of layers, filter sizes, and other design choices, and have achieved even better performance on image recognition tasks. For example, ResNet, developed by Kaiming He et al. in 2015, achieved a top-5 error rate of 3.6% on the ILSVRC challenge, surpassing human-level performance.

Overall, CNNs have revolutionized the field of computer vision, enabling machines to recognize and classify images with unprecedented accuracy. Their success has also paved the way for the development of deep learning algorithms in other domains, such as natural language processing and speech recognition.

Recurrent neural networks and natural language processing

Recurrent neural networks (RNNs) are a type of neural network that allows for sequential data processing. Unlike traditional neural networks, which take in fixed-size inputs, RNNs can take in inputs of varying lengths and sizes, making them useful for tasks such as natural language processing (NLP). RNNs are especially useful for tasks that involve predicting the next word or character in a sequence.

The basic idea behind RNNs is that they maintain a "hidden state" that represents the network's "memory" of previous inputs. This hidden state is updated at each time step based on the current input and the previous hidden state. In this way, the network can learn to "remember" information from previous inputs and use it to inform its predictions.

One popular type of RNN is the long short-term memory (LSTM) network. LSTMs were developed to address the problem of vanishing gradients, which occurs when the gradients used to update the network's weights become very small and cause the network to stop learning. LSTMs use a set of gates to control the flow of information into and out of the hidden state, which helps to mitigate the vanishing gradient problem.

In NLP, RNNs and LSTMs are used for a variety of tasks, including language modeling, machine translation, and sentiment analysis. Language modeling involves predicting the next word in a sentence given the previous words, while machine translation involves translating text from one language to another. Sentiment analysis involves determining the emotional tone of a piece of text, such as whether a review is positive or negative.

Overall, RNNs and LSTMs have been instrumental in advancing the field of NLP and have enabled significant progress in tasks such as machine translation and language modeling. However, they are still limited in their ability to understand the deeper meaning and context of language, and researchers continue to work on developing more sophisticated models for NLP tasks.

Reinforcement learning and game playing

Reinforcement learning is a subfield of machine learning that deals with how an agent can learn to make decisions by interacting with an environment. The agent receives rewards or penalties based on its actions, and its goal is to learn the optimal sequence of actions that maximize its reward over time. Reinforcement learning has been successfully applied to various domains, including robotics, finance, and game playing.

Game playing has long been a popular research topic in artificial intelligence, with the goal of developing programs that can play games at a superhuman level. One of the earliest successful examples of game playing with reinforcement learning was TD-Gammon, a backgammon playing program developed by Tesauro in 1992. TD-Gammon used a neural network to evaluate board positions and was trained using reinforcement learning. Despite its simplicity, TD-Gammon was able to achieve a level of play that surpassed the world champion at the time.

In recent years, reinforcement learning has been used to develop agents that can play complex games such as Go and chess at a superhuman level. In 2016, AlphaGo, a program developed by Google DeepMind, defeated the world champion in the game of Go. AlphaGo used a combination of deep neural networks and reinforcement learning to learn to play the game. The program was trained by playing against itself and was able to discover new strategies that human players had not previously considered.

Another example of reinforcement learning in game playing is the OpenAI Five, a team of five agents that can play the game Dota 2 at a superhuman level. OpenAI Five was trained using deep reinforcement learning and played against human players in a tournament, where it was able to defeat some of the world's best players.

Reinforcement learning has also been used to develop agents that can play Atari games at a superhuman level. In 2013, Mnih et al. developed the deep Q-network (DQN), which used a neural network to learn to play Atari games from raw pixels. DQN was trained using reinforcement learning and was able to achieve human-level performance on several Atari games.

Reinforcement learning has the potential to revolutionize many fields, including robotics, finance, and healthcare. For example, reinforcement learning can be used to develop robots that can learn to perform complex tasks such as assembly and manipulation, or to optimize financial portfolios. In healthcare, reinforcement learning can be used to develop personalized treatment plans for patients with chronic diseases.

However, reinforcement learning also presents several challenges. One of the main challenges is the problem of exploration versus exploitation, where the agent must balance the need to explore new actions with the need to exploit actions that have previously yielded high rewards. Another challenge is the problem of credit assignment, where the agent must correctly assign credit to its actions in order to learn the optimal sequence of actions. These challenges have spurred ongoing research in reinforcement learning and are the subject of many current research efforts.

In conclusion, reinforcement learning is a subfield of machine learning that deals with how an agent can learn to make decisions by interacting with an environment. It has been successfully applied to various domains, including game playing, robotics, finance, and healthcare. Reinforcement learning has the potential to revolutionize many fields, but also presents several challenges that are the subject of ongoing research.

Chapter 4: The Dark Side of AI
Potential risks and challenges presented by AI

Artificial Intelligence (AI) has made tremendous strides in recent years, with its applications now permeating many aspects of our lives. From personal assistants on our smartphones to self-driving cars, AI has shown great potential in improving efficiency, accuracy, and convenience. However, as with any powerful technology, there are also potential risks and challenges that need to be considered. In fact, a whole book could be written about the potential downsides of AI.

In this chapter, we will provide an overview of some of the most pressing concerns about the negative impacts of AI, while also referencing the book "Perils of Progress-Navigating Dark Sides of AI" to help the reader further explore this topic. Scan the QR code to get the book about dark sides here.

One of the most pressing concerns about the dark side of AI is the potential for job displacement. With the increasing automation of jobs, it is estimated that up to 47% of jobs in the United States are at risk of being automated in the coming decades. While some argue that AI will create new jobs, it is unclear whether these new jobs will be enough to replace the ones lost. This could result in significant social and economic disruption, particularly for low-skilled workers.

Another concern is the potential for biased decision-making by AI algorithms. AI systems learn from the data they are trained on, and if that data is biased, the AI system can perpetuate that bias. This has already been seen in the case of facial recognition systems, which have been shown to be less accurate in recognizing people with darker skin tones. This bias could also be present in other decision-making systems, such as those used for hiring, lending, and criminal justice, leading to discriminatory outcomes.

Privacy is another concern when it comes to AI. As AI systems collect more and more data about us, there is a risk that this data could be misused or abused. For example, data collected by smart home devices could be used by burglars to identify when a home is empty, or data collected by health trackers could be used by insurance companies to adjust premiums. There are also concerns about government surveillance using AI systems, particularly in countries with authoritarian regimes.

AI systems also have the potential to be used for malicious purposes, such as cyberattacks or weaponization. Malicious actors could use AI to create more sophisticated and effective attacks, or to develop autonomous weapons that could be used without human intervention. This could lead to a destabilization of international security, particularly if these weapons fall into the hands of non-state actors.

Finally, there is the concern of AI systems becoming too powerful and uncontrollable. As AI becomes more advanced and capable, it could potentially become impossible to predict or control its behavior. This could lead to unintended consequences, such as an AI system taking actions that are harmful to humans or society as a whole. This has been referred to as the "control problem" in AI, and is a topic of ongoing research and debate in the field.

In conclusion, while AI has tremendous potential to improve our lives, it is also important to consider the potential risks and challenges that it presents. The book "Perils of Progress-Navigating Dark Sides of AI" provides a comprehensive exploration of these issues and is recommended for further reading on this important topic.

Job displacement and automation

Introduction: As the field of Artificial Intelligence (AI) continues to advance, concerns about job displacement and automation have become more prominent. With the rise of automation and intelligent machines, many people are worried about the impact on employment and the economy as a whole. In this chapter, we will explore the potential risks and challenges presented by AI in terms of job displacement and automation.

Job Displacement: One of the most immediate and tangible effects of AI is job displacement. Automation has already begun to replace human workers in many industries, including manufacturing, transportation, and retail. As AI technology continues to improve, more and more jobs are likely to become automated, leading to even more job losses. According to a report by the World Economic Forum, over 75 million jobs worldwide could be displaced by automation by 2022.

One concern is that the jobs most at risk of displacement are low-skilled and low-wage jobs. These jobs are often held by vulnerable populations, including women, minorities, and workers in developing countries. As these jobs are replaced by machines, it could exacerbate existing social and economic inequalities.

On the other hand, some experts argue that AI could create new jobs and industries that do not exist today. For example, as more jobs become automated, there may be an increased demand for workers with expertise in AI, robotics, and automation. However, it remains to be seen whether the new jobs created will be enough to offset the number of jobs lost to automation.

Automation: In addition to job displacement, AI and automation also present challenges related to the nature of work itself. As more tasks become automated, workers may find that their jobs become more routine and less fulfilling. This could lead to increased dissatisfaction and even mental health issues.

Another concern is that the rise of automation could exacerbate income inequality. The benefits of automation are likely to accrue to those who own and control the technology, while low-skilled workers are more likely to be displaced. This could lead to increased economic inequality and social unrest.

Finally, there is a concern that AI could be used to automate decision-making processes that are currently done by humans. This could lead to a loss of transparency and accountability in decision-making, as well as potential biases that are programmed into the algorithms.

Conclusion: AI and automation have the potential to revolutionize many industries and improve our lives in countless ways. However, they also present significant risks and challenges related to job displacement and automation. As we continue to develop and deploy AI technology, it is important to carefully consider the potential consequences and take steps to mitigate any negative impacts. This may include investing in education and training programs to prepare workers for the jobs of the future, ensuring that AI is designed and deployed in a way that is transparent and accountable, and considering policies such as a universal basic income to mitigate the potential economic impacts of automation.

Bias in AI decision-making

AI systems have the potential to improve decision-making in various areas, such as healthcare, finance, and criminal justice. However, AI systems are only as good as the data they are trained on. If the data is biased, the AI system will also be biased, leading to unfair or discriminatory outcomes. In this chapter, we will explore the issue of bias in AI decision-making, its causes, and its consequences. We will also examine potential solutions and best practices to mitigate the impact of bias in AI systems.

The problem of bias in AI decision-making:

AI algorithms are designed to learn from data, and the quality of the data is critical for the performance of the algorithm. If the data is biased, the AI algorithm will be biased as well. For instance, if an AI algorithm is trained on historical data that reflects past discrimination, such as gender or racial bias, the algorithm will reproduce this bias in its predictions or recommendations. This can result in unfair treatment of individuals or groups and perpetuate existing inequalities.

There are several sources of bias in AI decision-making, including:

1. Data bias: This occurs when the training data used to train the AI algorithm is not representative of the

population it is intended to serve. For example, if an AI algorithm is trained on data that is predominantly male, it may not perform well for female users.

2. Algorithmic bias: This occurs when the AI algorithm itself is biased due to the design of the algorithm or the assumptions it makes. For example, if an AI algorithm is designed to identify high-risk patients for a certain disease based on their medical history, it may overlook patients from certain racial or ethnic backgrounds due to the assumptions made by the algorithm.

3. Human bias: This occurs when the individuals responsible for designing or implementing the AI system introduce their own biases consciously or unconsciously. For example, if the people designing an AI system come from a homogenous background, they may not consider the needs of a diverse user base.

The consequences of bias in AI decision-making:

The consequences of bias in AI decision-making can be severe, including perpetuating existing inequalities, reinforcing stereotypes, and violating individuals' rights. For example, a biased AI algorithm used in the criminal justice system could result in the overrepresentation of certain racial or ethnic groups in the criminal justice system, perpetuating racial disparities. Similarly, a biased AI algorithm used in hiring could perpetuate gender or racial discrimination, resulting in unfair treatment of individuals.

Solutions to mitigate the impact of bias in AI systems:

There are several solutions to mitigate the impact of bias in AI systems. These include:

1. Diverse representation: Having diverse teams of designers, developers, and testers can help identify and mitigate potential biases in AI systems.

2. Data quality: Ensuring that the training data used to train AI systems is representative of the population it is intended to serve can help mitigate data bias.

3. Algorithmic transparency: Making AI algorithms transparent and explainable can help identify and mitigate algorithmic bias.

4. Continuous monitoring: Continuously monitoring AI systems for bias and performance can help identify and correct issues before they become problematic.

5. Fairness metrics: Using fairness metrics to measure the impact of AI systems on different groups can help identify and correct biases in AI systems.

Conclusion:

AI systems have the potential to improve decision-making in various areas, but they are only as good as the data they are trained on. Bias in AI decision-making can result in unfair treatment of individuals or groups and perpetuate existing inequalities. However, there are solutions to mitigate the impact of bias in AI systems, including diverse representation, data quality, algorithmic transparency, continuous monitoring, and fairness metrics. As AI systems become more prevalent in our society, it is essential to address the issue of bias in AI decision-making to ensure that these systems are fair and just for everyone. In addition, the development and implementation of ethical frameworks for AI can guide the responsible use of these technologies and prevent harm. It is important for AI developers, policymakers, and users to work together to create and enforce ethical standards that prioritize fairness and transparency in AI decision-making. By doing so, we can maximize the benefits of AI while minimizing its potential negative consequences.

Privacy and security concerns

Introduction The increasing use of AI technology raises concerns about data privacy and security. As AI systems rely on large amounts of data to train their models, the data they collect and process can pose significant risks to individuals and organizations. In this section, we will discuss the privacy and security concerns associated with AI and the potential solutions to address these challenges.

Privacy Concerns

Data Collection and Usage AI systems require massive amounts of data to learn and improve their performance. However, this data can be sensitive and personal, including information about individuals' behavior, preferences, and even biometric data. AI systems can collect data from various sources, including social media, sensors, and other IoT devices. This data can be used to train models that can analyze and predict human behavior, which can be used for various purposes, including targeted advertising, surveillance, and even manipulating people's opinions.

Data Storage and Protection Storing large amounts of data in centralized databases can increase the risk of data breaches and unauthorized access. AI systems often store data in the cloud, where it can be accessed by multiple parties. Additionally, AI systems can be vulnerable to cyber-attacks, such as hacking and malware, which can compromise the confidentiality, integrity, and availability of the data.

Legal and Ethical Considerations AI systems can also violate privacy laws and ethical principles, especially when dealing with sensitive data. In some cases, AI systems can make decisions based on protected characteristics, such as race, gender, and age, leading to discriminatory outcomes. Additionally, some AI systems may violate the principle of informed consent, where individuals must be informed about the collection and use of their data.

Security Concerns

Cybersecurity Threats As AI systems become more prevalent, they become attractive targets for cybercriminals. AI systems can be vulnerable to various cyber-attacks, including malware, phishing, and denial-of-service attacks. Additionally, AI systems can be used to launch cyber-attacks, including automated hacking, social engineering, and botnets.

AI Malfunctions and Misuse AI systems can malfunction, leading to unintended consequences, including security breaches and system failures. Additionally, AI systems can be intentionally misused for malicious purposes, including cyber-attacks, fraud, and identity theft. As AI systems become more autonomous, they can make decisions that can have significant impacts on individuals and organizations.

Solutions

Privacy and security concerns associated with AI require comprehensive solutions that consider technical, legal, and ethical factors. Here are some potential solutions to address these challenges:

Privacy Solutions

- Data minimization: AI systems should collect only the necessary data to train their models and avoid collecting sensitive information that can identify individuals.

- Privacy by design: AI systems should be designed with privacy in mind, including privacy-preserving techniques such as differential privacy, homomorphic encryption, and secure multi-party computation.

- Data protection: AI systems should store data in secure locations and use encryption and access controls to protect data from unauthorized access.

- Transparency: AI systems should be transparent about their data collection and usage practices and provide individuals with the right to access and control their data.

Security Solutions

- Cybersecurity: AI systems should be designed with security in mind, including secure coding practices, regular security testing, and the use of security frameworks and standards.

- Explainability: AI systems should be transparent about their decision-making processes, including the data and algorithms used to make decisions.

- Governance and regulation: AI systems should be subject to regulatory frameworks that ensure their ethical and legal use and prevent misuse and abuse.

- Continuous monitoring: AI systems should be continuously monitored for security breaches, data misuse, and ethical violations.

Conclusion

AI systems have enormous potential to transform society positively, but they also pose significant privacy and security risks. The potential misuse of sensitive data, cyber-attacks, and AI malfunctions can lead to severe consequences such as identity theft, financial loss, and damage to critical infrastructure. One major concern is the collection, storage, and use of personal data by AI systems. As AI systems become more sophisticated, they can collect large amounts of data, including personal and sensitive information. This data can be used to make decisions that could impact individuals' lives, such as credit scoring, job hiring, and medical diagnoses. Additionally, AI systems can be vulnerable to cyber-attacks, which can compromise the confidentiality and integrity of the data they handle. There is also a risk of AI malfunctions, which can lead to unintended consequences such as autonomous vehicles causing accidents. Therefore, it is crucial to ensure that AI systems are designed with strong privacy and security protections, including data encryption, access control, and regular system testing and updates. Additionally, regulations and standards must be put in place to ensure that AI systems do not violate individuals' privacy rights or pose security risks.

Chapter 5: The Societal Impact of AI

The impact of AI on employment and the economy

Artificial Intelligence (AI) has the potential to revolutionize the way we work, but it also has the potential to cause significant disruptions in the employment landscape. In recent years, there has been a growing concern about the impact of AI on employment and the economy. While some experts predict that AI will lead to the creation of new jobs and higher productivity, others argue that it will lead to mass job displacement and a widening of economic inequality. This chapter will explore the potential impact of AI on employment and the economy.

The impact of AI on employment:

AI has already begun to impact the labor market, with automation replacing many jobs in manufacturing, transportation, and customer service. The most significant impact has been felt in low-skill and routine jobs, which are most easily automated. As AI technology continues to advance, it is likely that more jobs will be affected, including those in finance, healthcare, and professional services.

However, not all experts agree that AI will lead to widespread job displacement. Some argue that AI will create new jobs in areas such as AI research, programming, and maintenance. AI may also increase productivity and lead to the development of new products and services, which could create new jobs.

The impact of AI on the economy:

The impact of AI on the economy is a complex issue, and it is difficult to predict the full extent of its effects. On the one hand, AI has the potential to increase productivity, reduce costs, and create new products and services, which could lead to economic growth. On the other hand, if AI leads to significant job displacement, it could lead to a decrease in consumer spending and a widening of economic inequality.

There is also a concern that AI could exacerbate existing inequalities in the economy. For example, if AI leads to a concentration of wealth and power in the hands of a small group of individuals or corporations, it could lead to a widening of the wealth gap between the rich and poor.

Policy responses:

To address the potential impact of AI on employment and the economy, policymakers will need to take a proactive approach. One potential response is to invest in education and training programs to help workers acquire the skills needed to work alongside AI systems. This could include programs in computer science, data analysis, and problem-solving.

Another potential response is to provide income support and retraining programs for workers who are displaced by AI. This could include job retraining programs, unemployment benefits, and wage subsidies.

Policymakers could also consider implementing regulations to ensure that AI systems are developed and deployed in a way that is fair and equitable. This could include regulations around data privacy, algorithmic transparency, and bias detection and mitigation.

Conclusion:

AI has the potential to transform the way we work and live, but it also presents significant challenges for employment and the economy. While some experts predict that AI will lead to new jobs and higher productivity, others are concerned about the potential for mass job displacement and widening economic inequality. Policymakers will need to take a proactive approach to ensure that the benefits of AI are shared widely and that the negative impacts are mitigated.

AI in education and healthcare

AI in education and healthcare is a rapidly growing field that has the potential to revolutionize the way we learn and receive medical care. From personalized learning to precision medicine, AI is transforming these industries in ways that were once thought impossible. In this section, we will explore the impact of AI on education and healthcare and how it is changing the way we approach these critical areas.

AI in Education:

AI has the potential to personalize learning and provide tailored education to each student, regardless of their background or learning style. Through the use of machine learning algorithms and data analytics, AI can analyze student performance and adapt to their specific needs, providing feedback and resources that cater to their individual learning styles.

One example of this is adaptive learning, which uses AI to provide personalized learning experiences that adapt to a student's abilities and progress. Adaptive learning systems can use data from student performance, such as their test scores and quiz results, to tailor learning activities and resources that fit their learning style and pace.

AI can also be used to enhance educational content, such as through the use of chatbots or virtual assistants. These tools can answer student questions, provide feedback on assignments, and offer personalized recommendations for further learning.

Additionally, AI can help bridge the digital divide and provide access to education for underserved communities. Through the use of AI-powered mobile apps, online courses, and other digital learning tools, students can receive quality education regardless of their location or socio-economic status.

AI in Healthcare:

AI is also transforming the healthcare industry, offering new opportunities to improve patient outcomes, enhance clinical decision-making, and lower costs. AI is being used in a wide range of applications in healthcare, from disease diagnosis and treatment to drug development and clinical research.

One key area where AI is making a significant impact is in precision medicine. By using machine learning algorithms to analyze large sets of patient data, researchers and clinicians can identify patterns and insights that can lead to more accurate and personalized treatments. For example, AI can help identify specific genetic mutations that may be driving a patient's cancer, enabling doctors to develop targeted therapies that can more effectively treat the disease.

AI is also being used to enhance medical imaging, such as through the use of computer-aided diagnosis (CAD) systems. CAD systems can analyze medical images and help detect abnormalities or lesions that may be missed by human radiologists. This can lead to earlier detection of diseases and better patient outcomes.

Another area where AI is being used in healthcare is in remote patient monitoring. By using wearable devices and other sensors, AI-powered systems can monitor patient health and provide early warning signs of potential health problems. This can lead to earlier interventions and improved patient outcomes.

Conclusion:

AI is rapidly transforming the way we approach education and healthcare. From personalized learning to precision medicine, AI is providing new opportunities to improve patient outcomes and enhance learning experiences. However, as with any new technology, there are also challenges and concerns that need to be addressed. Ensuring that AI is used in an ethical and responsible manner will be critical to realizing its full potential in these critical areas.

AI and social inequality

AI has the potential to bring about positive social change, but it also has the potential to widen the gap between the rich and the poor, exacerbate social inequalities, and reinforce existing power structures. In this section, we will examine the ways in which AI can contribute to social inequality.

One of the primary ways in which AI can contribute to social inequality is through biased decision-making. As we have already discussed, AI systems can be biased against certain groups of people, such as minorities or women, due to the data they are trained on. This bias can manifest itself in various ways, such as in hiring decisions, loan approvals, or criminal justice outcomes, leading to the perpetuation of existing inequalities.

Another way in which AI can contribute to social inequality is by exacerbating the digital divide. AI requires significant computational resources, and those who do not have access to these resources may be left behind. This can be particularly problematic for individuals living in impoverished or rural areas, where access to technology may be limited. Moreover, those who are unable to use or understand AI may miss out on job opportunities or other benefits that it provides, leading to further social inequality.

Additionally, the use of AI in recruitment, hiring, and job performance evaluations can lead to a reinforcement of gender and racial biases. For example, a company that uses an AI-based recruitment tool to screen resumes may inadvertently exclude women or individuals from certain ethnic backgrounds, as the algorithm may be trained on past data, which itself was biased. Similarly, an AI-based performance evaluation system may perpetuate existing biases in the way it evaluates employees, leading to inequitable compensation and promotion decisions.

Furthermore, AI can contribute to social inequality by creating new forms of work that are low-paying, insecure, and require little to no benefits. For example, the rise of the gig economy has created a range of new jobs that are dependent on AI-based platforms, such as ride-sharing and food delivery apps. While these jobs provide flexibility and convenience, they often come with low pay, no job security, and no benefits. This can contribute to a widening of the income gap and exacerbate existing social inequalities.

Finally, the use of AI in surveillance and policing can lead to increased discrimination and targeting of marginalized communities. For example, the use of facial recognition technology in law enforcement has been shown to be less accurate for people with darker skin tones, leading to a higher likelihood of misidentification and wrongful arrest. Additionally, predictive policing algorithms have been criticized for disproportionately targeting communities of color, perpetuating racial biases and leading to increased incarceration rates.

To mitigate the impact of AI on social inequality, it is essential to ensure that AI is developed and deployed in a way that is transparent, accountable, and equitable. This includes ensuring that AI systems are designed with diverse representation and that the data they are trained on is diverse and representative. It also involves developing fairness metrics to evaluate the impact of AI systems on different groups and continuously monitoring for bias. Furthermore, it requires policies and regulations that promote fair and equitable access to AI resources and ensure that AI-based decisions are transparent, explainable, and subject to human oversight. By addressing the issue of social inequality in AI, we can harness the power of this technology to bring about positive social change and reduce existing inequalities.

AI and the environment

Artificial intelligence (AI) has the potential to address many of the world's environmental challenges. The integration of AI into environmental systems can provide greater efficiency, precision, and analysis in managing natural resources, conserving biodiversity, and mitigating climate change. However, like any technology, AI also has its drawbacks and unintended consequences that need to be addressed to ensure that it promotes environmental sustainability.

AI for Environmental Monitoring and Management

One of the most promising applications of AI in the environment is for monitoring and managing natural resources. For example, AI can help monitor air and water quality, track changes in land use and deforestation, and identify areas at risk of natural disasters. By analyzing vast amounts of data from sensors, satellites, and other sources, AI can provide early warnings of potential environmental threats and enable proactive responses.

AI can also help optimize resource management and conservation efforts. For example, AI-powered precision agriculture can reduce the use of fertilizers and pesticides, optimize irrigation, and improve crop yields, thereby reducing the environmental impact of agriculture. Similarly,

AI can optimize energy use in buildings and cities, reducing greenhouse gas emissions and promoting energy efficiency.

AI for Climate Change Mitigation and Adaptation

AI can also play a significant role in mitigating and adapting to climate change. For instance, AI-powered climate modeling can provide accurate projections of future climate scenarios, helping policymakers make informed decisions about mitigation and adaptation strategies. AI can also be used to optimize renewable energy generation, such as wind and solar power, and to improve energy storage systems, making renewable energy more viable and cost-effective.

AI can also help reduce carbon emissions in transportation by optimizing traffic flow, reducing congestion, and improving public transportation systems. In addition, AI can assist in carbon capture and storage efforts by identifying suitable sites for carbon sequestration and monitoring the effectiveness of these efforts.

AI for Environmental Conservation and Biodiversity

AI can also contribute to efforts to conserve biodiversity and protect endangered species. For example, AI-powered cameras can identify and track animal species, allowing conservationists to monitor their movements and behavior. AI can also help identify and map habitats, which can inform conservation strategies and help protect endangered species.

AI can also assist in monitoring and reducing illegal activities such as poaching and illegal logging. By analyzing data from cameras, satellites, and other sources, AI can detect and track illegal activities, enabling law enforcement agencies to take timely action.

Challenges and Risks

Despite the many potential benefits of AI in environmental management, there are also several challenges and risks associated with its use. One of the main concerns is the energy consumption of AI systems, which can be significant, particularly in large-scale applications. The carbon footprint of AI systems can offset some of the potential benefits of their use, particularly if they rely on fossil fuels for energy.

Another concern is the accuracy and reliability of AI systems. AI relies on vast amounts of data to make decisions, and if the data is incomplete, biased, or inaccurate, it can lead to erroneous decisions. This is particularly relevant in environmental applications, where incomplete or inaccurate data can have significant consequences for biodiversity, ecosystems, and human health.

Moreover, AI systems can also be vulnerable to cyberattacks, which can compromise their accuracy and integrity. In environmental applications, cyberattacks can have severe consequences, such as the manipulation of data that leads to incorrect decisions or the release of hazardous substances.

Lastly, the use of AI in environmental management can also raise ethical concerns, particularly regarding the impact on human rights and social justice. The use of AI to manage natural resources can lead to the displacement of local communities, the violation of indigenous rights, and the exploitation of vulnerable populations.

Conclusion

AI has the potential to transform the way we manage and protect the environment. From the use of drones to monitor wildlife populations to the optimization of energy usage through smart grids, AI can help us address environmental challenges more efficiently and effectively. However, as with any technology, there are also risks and challenges associated with the use of AI for environmental purposes. It is essential to address these challenges, such as data privacy concerns and potential unintended consequences of AI-driven decisions, to ensure that we use AI to support environmental sustainability responsibly. By embracing a multidisciplinary approach that involves experts from various fields, we can harness the full potential of AI to address the pressing environmental challenges facing our planet today. Ultimately, the responsible and ethical use of AI in environmental applications can help us achieve a more sustainable and equitable future for all.

Chapter 6: The Ethical Implications of AI

The ethical and moral implications of AI

The emergence and proliferation of AI has raised important ethical and moral questions, as the technology becomes increasingly intertwined with everyday life. As AI systems continue to advance in their capabilities, it is crucial to examine the ethical implications of their use.

One of the most significant ethical concerns surrounding AI is the potential for machines to make decisions that have a profound impact on human lives. As AI becomes more advanced and autonomous, it raises questions about the responsibility and accountability of those who create and use the technology. For example, if an AI system makes a decision that harms someone, who should be held responsible: the machine, its designers, or its users?

Another major ethical concern is the potential for AI to exacerbate existing social and economic inequalities. AI systems can be trained on biased data, perpetuating and even amplifying discriminatory practices. Additionally, as AI systems replace human workers in certain industries, it raises questions about the distribution of wealth and power in society.

Furthermore, AI has the potential to disrupt fundamental moral principles, such as privacy and autonomy. The ability of AI to process vast amounts of data and make predictions based on that data raises questions about individual privacy and the right to control one's own personal information. Additionally, the use of AI in decision-making can reduce the agency of individuals, as the technology is designed to predict and influence behavior.

In addition to these concerns, there are also broader ethical considerations related to the development and use of AI. For example, it is important to consider the potential environmental impacts of the massive energy consumption required to train and run AI systems. Additionally, there are questions about the use of AI in warfare and the potential for the technology to be used for malicious purposes.

To address these ethical concerns, it is important to establish clear ethical guidelines and standards for the development and use of AI. This includes ensuring that AI systems are transparent and explainable, so that their decision-making processes can be understood and audited. Additionally, it is crucial to promote diversity and inclusivity in the development of AI systems, to avoid perpetuating existing inequalities.

Finally, it is important to engage in ongoing dialogue and reflection about the ethical implications of AI, as the technology continues to evolve and become more integrated into society. This includes involving a wide range of stakeholders in the discussion, including policymakers, industry leaders, and members of the public. By engaging in this ongoing dialogue, we can ensure that the development and use of AI is ethical, responsible, and aligned with our fundamental moral values.

Bias and fairness in AI decision-making

Introduction: As artificial intelligence (AI) is increasingly being used to make decisions that impact human lives, it has become essential to consider the ethical implications of these decisions. One of the critical ethical issues in AI is bias and fairness in decision-making. Bias in AI decision-making can result in unfair treatment of individuals or groups and perpetuate existing inequalities. This article will explore the causes and consequences of bias in AI decision-making, and discuss some potential solutions to address these issues.

Causes of Bias in AI Decision-making: Bias in AI decision-making can arise from several sources, including biased data, biased algorithms, and biased human decision-making. Biased data can occur when the data used to train an AI system is not representative of the population it is meant to serve, or when the data reflects existing biases in society. Biased algorithms can occur when the design of the algorithm or the parameters used to train it reflects the biases of the developers. Finally, biased human decision-making can occur when the people designing or using the AI system have their biases that influence its use.

Consequences of Bias in AI Decision-making: The consequences of bias in AI decision-making can be severe and far-reaching. For example, biased algorithms used in hiring processes can result in discrimination against individuals from certain racial or ethnic groups, leading to a lack of diversity in the workforce. Similarly, biased algorithms used in criminal justice systems can result in harsher treatment of individuals from certain racial or ethnic groups, perpetuating existing biases in the justice system. Finally, biased algorithms used in financial decision-making can result in unequal access to credit and investment opportunities.

Solutions to Address Bias in AI Decision-making: Several potential solutions can help mitigate the impact of bias in AI decision-making, including diverse representation, data quality, algorithmic transparency, continuous monitoring, and fairness metrics. Diverse representation involves ensuring that the data used to train AI systems is representative of the population it is meant to serve, including people from diverse backgrounds. Data quality involves ensuring that the data used to train AI systems is accurate and free from biases. Algorithmic transparency involves making the algorithms used in AI decision-making more transparent, so that the decision-making process can be more easily understood and scrutinized. Continuous monitoring involves regularly monitoring AI systems for signs of bias or other ethical issues. Finally, fairness metrics involve measuring the impact of AI decision-making on different groups to ensure that the system is fair for everyone.

Conclusion: In conclusion, bias in AI decision-making is a significant ethical issue that must be addressed to ensure that AI systems are used in a fair and just manner. While several potential solutions exist, it is essential to continue researching and developing new approaches to ensure that AI systems are used ethically and fairly. By addressing these issues, we can unlock the full potential of AI to improve the lives of people around the world.

The role of humans in AI decision-making

The development of AI has raised important ethical questions about the role of humans in decision-making. As AI systems become more sophisticated and integrated into various aspects of society, it is essential to consider the extent to which humans should be involved in the decision-making process.

One of the primary concerns about AI is the potential for it to make decisions that have significant consequences for individuals or society as a whole. The fear is that AI systems may make decisions that are unfair or biased, leading to negative outcomes for certain groups. To mitigate these risks, it is necessary to involve humans in the decision-making process, either by providing oversight or by incorporating human input into the algorithms that govern the AI system.

One way to involve humans in AI decision-making is through the use of human-in-the-loop (HITL) systems. HITL systems incorporate human input into the decision-making process, allowing humans to provide feedback and override the decisions made by the AI system when necessary. HITL systems can be used in various applications, such as medical diagnosis, financial analysis, and self-driving cars, where it is critical to ensure that the AI system is making decisions that are fair and ethical.

Another way to involve humans in AI decision-making is through the use of explainable AI (XAI). XAI systems are designed to provide explanations for the decisions made by the AI system, allowing humans to understand the reasoning behind the decisions. This approach can be particularly useful in applications where decisions made by AI systems have significant consequences, such as in healthcare or criminal justice.

However, the involvement of humans in AI decision-making also raises ethical questions. For example, there is a concern that humans may introduce their biases and prejudices into the decision-making process, which could lead to unfair or discriminatory outcomes. Additionally, there is a risk that humans may abdicate their responsibility and defer too much to the AI system, leading to an erosion of human agency.

To address these ethical concerns, it is necessary to strike a balance between human oversight and AI autonomy. One approach is to ensure that the AI system is designed to operate within specific ethical and moral frameworks, which reflect the values of society as a whole. For example, an AI system used in healthcare could be designed to prioritize patient welfare, while an AI system used in criminal justice could be designed to prioritize fairness and impartiality.

Another approach is to ensure that humans are trained to understand and interact with AI systems in an ethical and responsible manner. This approach involves educating individuals about the limitations and capabilities of AI systems and teaching them how to use these systems in a way that is consistent with ethical principles.

In conclusion, the role of humans in AI decision-making is a complex and multifaceted issue that requires careful consideration. While the involvement of humans is necessary to ensure that AI systems are fair and ethical, it is essential to strike a balance between human oversight and AI autonomy. By designing AI systems to operate within specific ethical and moral frameworks and educating individuals about the responsible use of AI, we can ensure that AI technology is used to promote the greater good of society.

The ethics of creating autonomous AI systems

Introduction: The development of autonomous AI systems raises ethical concerns about their potential impact on society. Autonomous AI systems can operate independently of human control, which raises the question of who is responsible for their actions. This chapter explores the ethical implications of creating autonomous AI systems, including the potential risks and benefits, ethical concerns about responsibility and accountability, and the role of ethical frameworks in guiding their development.

Potential Benefits of Autonomous AI Systems: Autonomous AI systems have the potential to revolutionize many fields, including transportation, healthcare, and manufacturing. They can improve efficiency, reduce costs, and increase safety. In transportation, autonomous vehicles can reduce traffic accidents caused by human error, while in healthcare, they can improve patient outcomes by enabling faster and more accurate diagnoses. In manufacturing, autonomous systems can optimize production lines and reduce waste.

Ethical Concerns about Responsibility and Accountability: One of the main ethical concerns surrounding autonomous AI systems is the issue of responsibility and accountability. As these systems operate independently of human control, it is unclear who should be held responsible for their actions. This raises questions about legal liability and the allocation of responsibility between the designers, manufacturers, and users of these systems.

The Role of Ethical Frameworks in Guiding the Development of Autonomous AI Systems: To address the ethical concerns surrounding autonomous AI systems, various ethical frameworks have been proposed. One such framework is the principle of beneficence, which requires that autonomous AI systems be designed to maximize benefits and minimize harms. Another framework is the principle of non-maleficence, which requires that autonomous AI systems be designed to avoid doing harm to humans.

The Ethics of Programming Autonomous AI Systems: There are also ethical concerns about the programming of autonomous AI systems. The decisions made by these systems can have far-reaching consequences, and it is essential that they are programmed to act ethically. This raises questions about the development of ethical algorithms and the ethical training of AI systems.

The Potential Risks of Autonomous AI Systems: Despite the potential benefits, autonomous AI systems also pose significant risks. These systems can malfunction, make errors, or be hacked, potentially causing harm to individuals or society as a whole. There is also the risk that autonomous AI systems could be programmed to act in ways that are harmful to humans or violate ethical principles.

Conclusion: The development of autonomous AI systems raises significant ethical concerns, including issues of responsibility and accountability, the role of ethical frameworks in guiding development, and the potential risks and benefits of these systems. To ensure that the development of autonomous AI systems is ethical and responsible, it is essential to develop robust ethical frameworks and guidelines for their development and use. By doing so, we can harness the potential of these systems while minimizing their risks and ensuring their ethical and responsible use.

Conclusion

The potential future of AI and its impact on society

As AI continues to advance, its impact on society is expected to grow significantly. AI has the potential to transform various sectors, including healthcare, transportation, education, and the environment. However, it also raises ethical, moral, and societal challenges that need to be addressed to ensure its responsible use.

One of the most significant areas where AI is expected to have a massive impact is healthcare. AI can help healthcare providers diagnose diseases more accurately, develop personalized treatment plans, and reduce medical errors. For example, AI-powered diagnostic tools can analyze large amounts of medical data and provide insights to doctors, leading to earlier and more accurate diagnoses. Additionally, AI can help improve patient outcomes by identifying high-risk patients and providing preventative care.

AI is also expected to revolutionize transportation by enabling self-driving cars and trucks. Self-driving cars have the potential to reduce accidents caused by human error, reduce traffic congestion, and lower emissions by optimizing driving patterns. However, the widespread adoption of self-driving cars also raises ethical concerns, such as who is responsible in case of accidents or how to ensure the safety of passengers.

In education, AI can help personalize learning experiences for students and improve the effectiveness of teaching. AI-powered tools can analyze student performance data and provide recommendations for individualized learning plans. However, the use of AI in education also raises concerns about student privacy and how to ensure that AI is used in a way that benefits all students, regardless of their socioeconomic background.

AI can also play a critical role in protecting the environment. AI-powered sensors and monitoring systems can help detect pollution levels, track climate change, and protect wildlife. Additionally, AI can help optimize energy usage and reduce waste by identifying areas of inefficiency.

However, the widespread adoption of AI also raises ethical and moral concerns. One of the most significant concerns is the potential for AI to reinforce existing biases and inequalities. For example, if AI is trained on biased data, it may produce biased outcomes that discriminate against certain groups. Additionally, the rise of autonomous AI systems raises questions about the role of humans in decision-making and accountability for actions taken by AI systems.

As AI continues to advance, it is essential to ensure its responsible use and address the ethical, moral, and societal challenges that arise. This requires collaboration among governments, industry leaders, and experts in various fields to develop ethical frameworks and guidelines for the development and use of AI. It also requires continuous monitoring and evaluation of AI systems to ensure that they align with ethical standards and do not harm society.

In conclusion, AI has the potential to transform society in significant ways, but it also raises ethical, moral, and societal challenges that need to be addressed. The responsible development and use of AI require collaboration and coordination among various stakeholders to ensure that AI benefits society while minimizing its potential risks. The future of AI is bright, but it requires a thoughtful and proactive approach to ensure its responsible use.

The need for continued research and development in AI

The field of artificial intelligence (AI) has experienced remarkable growth over the last few decades, and it shows no signs of slowing down. As the technology continues to evolve and become more complex, it is crucial that we continue to invest in research and development to ensure that it is being used in the best way possible.

One of the main reasons why continued research and development is necessary is that the ethical and social implications of AI are still not fully understood. While AI has the potential to do a great deal of good, it also has the potential to cause harm if it is not used responsibly. For example, there are concerns about the potential for AI to be used to create autonomous weapons or to perpetuate social inequality. Continued research and development can help us to better understand these issues and to develop strategies to mitigate their impact.

Another reason why continued research and development is important is that AI has the potential to transform many different areas of society. For example, it has the potential to revolutionize healthcare, education, and transportation. By investing in research and development, we can ensure that these transformative technologies are being developed in a responsible and sustainable way.

Furthermore, continued research and development can help to ensure that AI is being developed in a way that is inclusive and accessible to everyone. Historically, technology has often been developed in ways that exclude certain groups of people, such as those with disabilities or those living in poverty. By investing in research and development, we can work to ensure that AI is being developed in a way that is inclusive and accessible to all.

In addition to the social and ethical implications of AI, there are also many technical challenges that need to be addressed. For example, current AI systems often lack the ability to explain their decisions, which can make it difficult to identify and correct errors. Continued research and development can help to address these technical challenges and to develop more robust and reliable AI systems.

Overall, the need for continued research and development in AI is clear. As the technology continues to evolve and become more complex, it is crucial that we invest in research and development to ensure that it is being used in the best way possible. By doing so, we can help to ensure that AI is being developed in a responsible and sustainable way that benefits society as a whole.

The importance of ethical and responsible AI development and use

As the field of AI continues to rapidly advance, it is crucial that researchers, developers, and policymakers prioritize ethical and responsible AI development and use. The potential benefits of AI are vast, but they must be balanced with the potential risks and negative consequences, particularly as AI systems become more prevalent in our society.

One of the key ethical considerations in AI development and use is the issue of bias and fairness. As discussed throughout this book, AI systems are only as good as the data they are trained on, and biased data can lead to biased outcomes that perpetuate existing societal inequalities. It is essential that AI systems are developed with diversity and inclusivity in mind, with diverse teams involved in their development and rigorous testing for bias and fairness.

Another critical ethical consideration is the impact of AI on employment and the economy. While AI has the potential to create new jobs and increase productivity, it can also lead to job displacement and exacerbate existing economic inequalities. It is essential that policymakers and businesses plan for the potential impact of AI on the workforce and ensure that individuals are prepared for the changes that AI may bring.

The use of AI in sensitive areas such as healthcare and criminal justice also requires careful ethical consideration. The potential benefits of AI in these areas are significant, but there are also risks associated with the use of AI, including the potential for bias, privacy concerns, and the possibility of harm to individuals. It is essential that the use of AI in these areas is guided by ethical principles and subject to rigorous oversight and regulation.

Finally, the potential future of AI is both exciting and uncertain. As AI systems become more advanced and capable, there is the potential for significant positive impact on society. However, there are also risks associated with the development of advanced AI, including the potential for unintended consequences and the possibility of the loss of human control over AI systems. It is crucial that researchers and policymakers continue to explore and understand the potential impact of AI on society, and prioritize ethical considerations in their development and use.

In conclusion, the development and use of AI must be guided by ethical and responsible principles to ensure that the potential benefits of AI are realized while minimizing the potential risks and negative consequences. The future of AI is exciting, but it is also uncertain, and it is essential that we approach it with a clear understanding of its potential impact on society and a commitment to ethical and responsible development and use.

Final thoughts and recommendations for further reading

As we have seen throughout this book, AI has the potential to transform many aspects of our lives, from healthcare and education to the environment and the economy. However, with this potential comes significant ethical and societal considerations, including privacy, bias, and the impact on employment and social inequality. As we continue to develop and integrate AI into our society, it is essential that we do so in a way that prioritizes ethical and responsible development and use.

One of the most critical steps in promoting ethical and responsible AI is education and awareness. It is important for policymakers, industry leaders, and the public to understand the implications of AI and the ethical considerations that need to be taken into account. This can involve developing educational programs and resources that promote a better understanding of AI and its ethical implications, as well as encouraging open and transparent communication about AI development and use.

Another important consideration is the need for ongoing research and development in AI. As AI continues to evolve and become more sophisticated, it is critical that we continue to invest in research that addresses ethical and societal considerations, as well as technical advancements. This can involve supporting interdisciplinary research that brings together experts in fields such as computer science, ethics, and social science to explore the implications of AI from multiple perspectives.

In addition, it is essential to prioritize diversity and inclusivity in AI development and use. This means ensuring that AI systems are developed and tested on diverse data sets that accurately represent the diversity of the population, as well as promoting the inclusion of diverse perspectives in AI development teams. This can help to mitigate the risk of bias and promote fair and equitable outcomes.

Finally, policymakers and industry leaders have a critical role to play in promoting ethical and responsible AI development and use. This can involve developing regulations and guidelines that promote transparency and accountability in AI development and use, as well as ensuring that AI is developed and used in a way that aligns with societal values and principles.

In conclusion, AI has the potential to transform many aspects of our lives, but it is critical that we prioritize ethical and responsible development and use. This can involve promoting education and awareness, investing in ongoing research and development, prioritizing diversity and inclusivity, and promoting transparent and accountable AI development and use. By doing so, we can help to ensure that AI benefits society as a whole and promotes a more equitable and just world.

For further reading, we recommend exploring academic journals and books on AI ethics, as well as resources provided by organizations such as the AI Now Institute, the Partnership on AI, and the IEEE Global Initiative on Ethics of Autonomous and Intelligent Systems. Additionally, staying up-to-date with industry news and developments can provide valuable insights into the latest advancements and trends in AI development and use.

THE END

Potential References

Introduction:

Russell, S. J., & Norvig, P. (2010). Artificial intelligence: A modern approach. Pearson Education.

Goodfellow, I., Bengio, Y., & Courville, A. (2016). Deep learning. MIT press.

Domingos, P. (2015). The master algorithm: How the quest for the ultimate learning machine will remake our world. Basic Books.

Chapter 1:

McCorduck, P. (2004). Machines who think: A personal inquiry into the history and prospects of artificial intelligence. AK Peters/CRC Press.

Crevier, D. (1993). AI: The tumultuous history of the search for artificial intelligence. Basic Books.

Nilsson, N. J. (2010). The quest for artificial intelligence: A history of ideas and achievements. Cambridge University Press.

Chapter 2:

Mitchell, T. (1997). Machine learning. McGraw Hill.

Alpaydin, E. (2010). Introduction to machine learning (2nd ed.). MIT Press.

Hastie, T., Tibshirani, R., & Friedman, J. (2009). The elements of statistical learning: Data mining, inference, and prediction (2nd ed.). Springer.

Chapter 3:

LeCun, Y., Bengio, Y., & Hinton, G. (2015). Deep learning. Nature, 521(7553), 436-444.

Goodfellow, I. J., Pouget-Abadie, J., Mirza, M., Xu, B., Warde-Farley, D., Ozair, S., ... & Bengio, Y. (2014). Generative adversarial nets. In Advances in neural information processing systems (pp. 2672-2680).

Schmidhuber, J. (2015). Deep learning in neural networks: An overview. Neural Networks, 61, 85-117.

Chapter 4:

Brynjolfsson, E., & McAfee, A. (2014). The second machine age: Work, progress, and prosperity in a time of brilliant technologies. WW Norton & Company.

Floridi, L., & Sanders, J. W. (Eds.). (2014). The philosophy of information. Oxford University Press.

Angwin, J., Larson, J., Mattu, S., & Kirchner, L. (2016). Machine bias. ProPublica, 23.

Chapter 5:

Brynjolfsson, E., Rock, D., & Syverson, C. (2018). Artificial intelligence and the modern productivity paradox: A clash of expectations and statistics. National Bureau of Economic Research.

Topol, E. J. (2019). Deep medicine: How artificial intelligence can make healthcare human again. Basic Books.

Noble, S. U. (2018). Algorithms of oppression: How search engines reinforce racism. NYU Press.

Chapter 6:

Bostrom, N. (2014). Superintelligence: Paths, dangers, strategies. Oxford University Press.

Taddeo, M. (2019). Ethics of artificial intelligence. Stanford Encyclopedia of Philosophy.

Russell, S. J. (2019). Human-compatible: Artificial intelligence and the problem of control. Viking.

Conclusion:

Floridi, L. (2019). The AI Revolution: Ethics, Power, and Justice. Oxford University Press.

Russell, S., & Norvig, P. (2020). Artificial Intelligence: A Modern Approach. Pearson.

Bostrom, N. (2014). Superintelligence: Paths, Dangers, Strategies. Oxford University Press.

Yampolskiy, R. V. (2016). Artificial Superintelligence: A Futuristic Approach. CRC Press.

Zeng, X., Chen, L., Lusch, R. F., & Li, S. (2021). Artificial intelligence: Opportunities and challenges in operations management. Journal of Operations Management, 69(1-2), 43-55.

Brynjolfsson, E., & Mitchell, T. (2017). What can machine learning do? Workforce implications. Science, 358(6370), 1530-1534.

Calvo, R. A., Deterding, S., Ryan, R. M., & Rigby, C. S. (2019). Health surveillance during interactive stress management training: A randomized trial. Applied Psychology: Health and Well-Being, 11(1), 137-162.

Taddeo, M., & Floridi, L. (2018). How AI can be a force for good. Science, 361(6404), 751-752.

Allen, C., & Wallach, W. (2014). Moral machines: Teaching robots right from wrong. Oxford University Press.

Hibbard, J. D. (2020). AI and ethics: Lessons learned. IEEE Transactions on Technology and Society, 1(1), 10-15.

www.ingramcontent.com/pod-product-compliance
Lightning Source LLC
LaVergne TN
LVHW021054100526
838202LV00083B/5850